EXPLORING WORLD CULTURES

Vietnam

Kaitlyn Duling

Cavendish
Square

New York

Published in 2019 by Cavendish Square Publishing, LLC
243 5th Avenue, Suite 136, New York, NY 10016

Copyright © 2019 by Cavendish Square Publishing, LLC

First Edition

Library of Congress Cataloging-in-Publication Data

Names: Duling, Kaitlyn, author.
Title: Vietnam / Kaitlyn Duling.
Description: New York: Cavendish Square, 2019. | Series: Exploring world cultures | Includes bibliographical references and index. | Audience: Grades 2-5.
Identifiers: LCCN 2017048059 (print) | LCCN 2017051367 (ebook) | ISBN 9781502638229 (library bound) | ISBN 9781502638236 (pbk.) | ISBN 9781502638243 (6 pack) | ISBN 9781502638250 (ebook)
Subjects: LCSH: Vietnam--Juvenile literature.
Classification: LCC DS556.39 (ebook) | LCC DS556.39 .D85 2018 (print) | DDC 959.7--dc23
LC record available at https://lccn.loc.gov/2017048059

Editorial Director: David McNamara
Editor: Jodyanne Benson
Copy Editor: Rebecca Rohan
Associate Art Director: Amy Greenan
Designer: Christina Shults
Production Coordinator: Karol Szymczuk
Photo Research: J8 Media

The photographs in this book are used by permission and through the courtesy of:
Cover, David Noton/Alamy Stock Photo; p. 5 hadynyah/istockphoto.com; p. 6 Peter Hermes Furian/Shutterstock.com; p. 7 Cuongvnd/Moment/Getty Images; p. 8 Pictures from History/Bridgeman Images; p. 9 Jorisvo/Shutterstock.com; p. 10 Maximumvector/Shutterstock.com; p. 11 Palis Michalis/Shutterstock.com; p. 12 Linh Pham/Getty Images; p. 13 Ben Jeayes/Shutterstock.com; p. 14 Trong Nguyen/Shutterstock.com; p. 15 Dragon Images/istockphoto.com; p. 16 vinhdav/istockphoto.com; p. 18 Nga Nguyen/Moment/Getty Images; p. 19 Dallas and John Heaton/Corbis/Getty Images; p. 20 calflier001 (http://www.flickr.com/people/28984065@N04)/File: Buddhist Temple Da Lat Vietnam JAN 2012 (7010701723).jpg/Wikimedia Commons; p. 21 Godong/Robert Harding/Getty Images; p. 22 Xita/Shutterstock.com; p. 24 Thoai/Shutterstock.com; p. 26 Longbao/istockphoto.com; p. 27 Gnomeandi/istockphoto.com; p. 28 Anna Pustynnikova/Shutterstock.com; p. 29 Tran Hai Duong (https://pixabay.com/users/JamesTran-3762406/)/File: Goi cuốn.jpg/Wikimedia Commons.

Printed in the United States of America

Contents

Introduction

Are you ready to explore Vietnam? You may have heard of this narrow country in southeastern Asia. You may have eaten yummy Vietnamese food. You have probably learned about the **civil wars** that were fought there. But did you know that Vietnam is so much more? It has rich **agriculture**. It has beautiful rivers and waterways.

What else would you see if you visited Vietnam? You would find mountains and tropical forests. You could also find yourself in a bustling city. Vietnam has a fascinating culture with beautiful art and music.

The capital of Vietnam is Hanoi. The city lies right along the Red River. It has a population of almost eight million people.

Vietnam has a long and interesting history. It is constantly growing and changing. There is so much to learn about the history of Vietnam and what it's like there today. Let's get started!

Boats are the main mode of transportation in the Mekong River Delta in Vietnam.

Geography

Vietnam is a long, thin country. It is tucked into the eastern part of Southeast Asia. It has a long coast along the South China Sea. It has cities and countryside. The north and south are very different! Southern Vietnam has a tropical climate. It is warm and wet. But the

Vietnam is a thin country with a very long coastline.

north is cooler and has only two seasons: cold and dry. Most of Vietnam has monsoon season.

FACT!

Vietnam is a little bigger than the state of New Mexico.

The River of Nine Dragons

The Mekong River runs through south Vietnam. It is long and splits off into nine smaller rivers. It is often called the River of Nine Dragons. The land around this river is called the delta. It makes good farmland. People grow rice there.

These are periods of intense rain. The north also has mountains, hills, and rivers. The south has the long Mekong River, swamps, and rice fields. Vietnam has beaches, islands, and more.

A long bridge crosses over the Mekong River in Ben Tre province.

People have lived in Vietnam for thousands of years. There were long dynasties of rule by different emperors. The country was independent but often at war with nearby peoples. For many hundreds of years, the country was

Gia Long was the first emperor of the Nguyen Dynasty.

under Chinese control. Southern Vietnam had many settlers from India. Both of these cultures influenced the area. In the 1800s, France took

Ho Chi Minh (1890–1969) was a **communist** leader who became prime minister and president of North Vietnam.

8

control. The people of Vietnam did not appreciate this. In 1945, the Vietnamese Communist Party took control of northern Vietnam. France kept control of the south. For decades, the two sides fought. China supported the North. The United States supported the South.

A portrait of communist leader Ho Chi Minh.

War

In the 1950s, the United States and China both got involved in a war between North and South Vietnam. It was a long and difficult war. In 1976, the two halves of Vietnam were joined under a single government.

9

Vietnam's official name is the Socialist Republic of Vietnam. Hanoi is the capital of Vietnam. Vietnam has a communist style of government. In a communist country, most things are shared and controlled by

The flag of Vietnam was designed in 1940.

the government. Even though this differs from the US government, it is still similar in some ways. Vietnam has its own constitution. It has a president and three branches. The branches include a body of lawmakers, the president, and the courts. Vietnam holds elections to choose members of the National Assembly. This is like our Congress. It also has a top court, much like our

Supreme Court. It is called the Supreme People's Court. There are many smaller courts within the system.

Hanoi is the capital city of Vietnam.

Party Time

The Communist Party of Vietnam is the only political party in the country. It is also called the CPV. The CPV was founded in 1930.

11

The Economy

Since its earliest days, Vietnam's economy has been based in agriculture. Rice, coffee, and rubber are all produced in the country. They are sold across the globe.

Coastal cities are very popular places with Chinese tourists.

Vietnam trades with other countries in Asia. It also trades with the United States, Australia, and the United Kingdom. Rice is the biggest crop. Vegetables, fruits, grains, and

FACT!

The money used in Vietnam is called the Vietnamese dong. Items are usually paid for in cash. Coins are discouraged.

sugarcane are grown there too. Vietnam also sells seafood, clothing, oil, coal, and more to other countries.

Vietnamese paper money is very colorful.

While many Vietnamese citizens farm the land, others work in business. Tourism is a large part of the economy in Vietnam. People take many vacations there. They come for the beaches, culture, and food.

Field or Forest?

Many of the crops in Vietnam are grown in fields. But, the country also grows crops in its forests. Cinnamon, bamboo, and more are grown in the forests.

Vietnam has started to see environmental changes. **Industry** is putting the water supply at risk. Waste from factories flows directly into rivers, dirtying the water. Modern industry also causes air pollution. Vietnam has some of the worst air quality

Work is being done to clean the polluted canals.

in the world. Many people wear masks to guard against the smoke and dust in the air. Over the

FACT!

In 2001, Vietnam began the National Strategy for Environmental Protection. This is a way to solve environmental problems, including pollution.

years, **deforestation** has been an ongoing issue in the country. This is the process of forests losing their trees. Deforestation can be caused by logging, fire, and war. The government has been working to replant and protect forests in recent years.

Face masks protect Vietnamese citizens from air pollution.

Agent Orange

During the Vietnam War, the United States sprayed a chemical called Agent Orange across the country to destroy plants that the enemy could hide in. Today, we know that this chemical causes serious health problems in humans. It remains in Vietnam's water and soil.

Vietnam is one of the most densely populated countries in the world. That means it has a large number of people per square mile. Vietnam is a relatively small country, but it has many people living in it.

These H'mong girls wear traditional dress during the Lunar New Year.

The population is over ninety million. Cities are especially crowded. In the 1980s, the Vietnamese government began encouraging people to move out of cities to reduce overcrowding.

The majority of people living in Vietnam belong to the Viet or Kinh ethnic group. These people are

descended from the country's original settlers. However, there are also over fifty ethnic minority groups. These groups and tribes are spread out across Vietnam, in the highlands and lowlands. There are Chinese groups, Hmong, Muong, Dao, and more.

What's in a Name?

The most popular surname (or last name) in Vietnam is Nguyen. Nearly half of all people have this surname! This does not mean they are related. It is just a very common name.

Lifestyle

Life in Vietnam is centered around family. When the Vietnamese speak of "family," though, they don't just mean immediate family. **Ancestors** are very important to Vietnamese

Family roles are very traditional in Vietnam.

culture. From a young age, children are taught to respect their elders and ancestors. It is important to honor the family name. In the family, the man

FACT!

Many Vietnamese women wear a *non la,* or a cone-shaped hat. This hat protects them from the sun.

works and provides money. The woman takes care of the home and family. She looks after the children and cares for her parents and in-laws. Wives might also work on the farm. Today, many women have jobs outside the home.

This young girl is wearing a non la.

A Loving Arrangement

In the past, most marriages were arranged. This means that parents would decide who their children would marry. Many brides and grooms would meet for the first time on the day of their engagement! Today, it is not uncommon to marry for love.

Religion

There is no single religion that most Vietnamese citizens follow. There are Christians, Buddhists, and more. The Catholic Church is very large in Vietnam. Christianity was brought by traders and made popular by French and American

Many Buddhist temples like this one can be found in Vietnam.

missionaries. **Buddhism** comes from India, but it is practiced by many people in Vietnam. The majority

FACT!

Officially, the Vietnamese government claims to uphold freedom of religion in the country. Since it is a communist country, this may look a little different than in other areas.

of Vietnamese citizens practice folk religions. These often involve worshipping ancestors, or those family members who were alive long ago. Sometimes these folk religions are combined with Buddhism. Temples and statues of Buddha can be found across the country.

There are Christian and Catholic churches in Vietnam, too.

Roman Catholicism in Vietnam

For many years, the Vietnamese government and the Roman Catholic Church have had a poor relationship. The Church remains anticommunist. The government closely controls the Catholic organizations within the country.

Language

The national language of Vietnam is—you guessed it—Vietnamese. There are Vietnamese speakers in Vietnam itself, as well as in nearby countries like Cambodia and Laos. It is

These daily newspapers are written in Vietnamese.

also spoken around the world. There are over a million Vietnamese speakers in the United States. There are many Vietnamese speakers in France, Australia, and the Czech Republic as well.

FACT!

In the United States, some students go to special language schools to learn Vietnamese.

ABCs in Vietnamese

When Vietnam was first settled, it didn't yet have its own alphabet. Vietnamese writing used Chinese characters. Over time, the alphabet changed. Today, it is uniquely Vietnamese.

If you grew up in Vietnam, you would speak Vietnamese. You might also speak French! Vietnam used to be a French colony. Today, many people speak both French and Vietnamese.

In school, children are taught Vietnamese. They are also taught French or English. Sometimes they learn both languages! Some students study Japanese or Korean. Learning languages is very important for the Vietnamese people.

The arts have a long history in Vietnam. Long-held traditions can include everything from painting on silk to making prints using carved woodblocks. The Vietnamese people enjoy a wide range of arts. Dance, theatre, and other performance arts are popular.

The Lunar New Year is a special annual holiday.

In addition to art, the Vietnamese also enjoy a range of festivals and holidays throughout

The Vietnamese New Year is called Tet. It is an important celebration of the arrival of spring.

Water Puppetry

Since the twelfth century, Vietnam has enjoyed a long history of water puppetry. In this tradition, puppets are attached to long poles hidden beneath a pool of water. There is a bamboo screen in front of the water. You can still see a water puppet show today!

the year. Many of these are based in ancient history. National Day celebrates the country's independence from France. Reunification Day marks the end of the Vietnam War. People also take part in Buddhist festivals, usually called pagoda festivals.

Fun and Play

Life in Vietnam is fun!
There are sports to play.
There is art and music.
The most popular sport
in Vietnam is soccer.
Other games and sports
are popular with kids
and adults. Many boys

These people are practicing martial arts in a city center.

and girls participate in **martial arts**. You may
have heard of karate or judo. Vietnam has its own

FACT!

In 2016, Vietnam participated in the
Summer Olympics in Rio de Janeiro, Brazil.
The country won its first gold medal in air
pistol, a shooting sport.

Some of Vietnam's most popular games are played with nets. Volleyball is very popular with both kids and adults. Badminton is also enjoyed by many people. Table tennis is often played, too!

varieties of martial arts. One of the most practiced is Binh Dinh. Other fun things to do in Vietnam include riding bicycles, singing karaoke, and playing card games. You can almost always find a game of chess or pool to play.

Bicycling is the main mode of transportation in many parts of Vietnam.

Food

If you love rice and noodles, you should try Vietnamese cuisine! Rice is grown all over Vietnam, so it is used in many dishes. Many noodles are actually made out of rice. A popular

Pho soup has a variety of different ingredients.

dish is pho, a hot soup made with rice noodles, meat, and spicy broth. It arrives in a big bowl. The soup is then topped with fresh herbs and sauces.

FACT!

One of the most popular flavors in Vietnam is something a little fishy—fish sauce! It is made from fermented fish and salt.

Where does it come from?

Vietnamese food has been influenced by food from around Europe. Some dishes use pâté, certain European meats and sauces, and even French rolls. You can also see Chinese and other Southeast Asian influences in Vietnamese cooking.

Some people consider pho to be the national dish of Vietnam. Other popular foods include spring rolls, stews, and banh mi (a sandwich made with crusty bread).

Spring rolls are made by rolling lettuce and other ingredients in rice paper.

29

Glossary

agriculture   The practice or science of farming.

ancestors   The people from which one is descended.

Buddhism   A religion that began in India that is based on the teachings of the Buddha.

civil war   A war between citizens residing in the same country.

communist   A way of organizing society in which property and resources are owned by the government.

deforestation   Removal of trees from logging, fires, or war.

industry   Any general business, manufacturing, or trade activity.

martial arts   Various sports that originated as a form of self-defense.

Find Out More

Books

Rau, Dana Meachen. *It's Cool to Learn about Countries: Vietnam*. Ann Arbor, MI: Cherry Lake Publishing, 2012.

Tran, Phuoc Thi Minh. *Vietnamese Children's Favorite Stories*. Clarendon, VT: Tuttle Publishing, 2015.

Website

Kid World Citizen: Vietnam

http://kidworldcitizen.org/category/asia/vietnam/

Video

National Geographic World Traveler: Vietnam

https://www.youtube.com/watch?v=AA58_NLs_ic

Index

About the Author

Kaitlyn Duling believes in the power of words to change hearts, minds, and, ultimately, actions. A poet, nonfiction author, and grant writer who grew up in Illinois, she now resides in Pittsburgh, Pennsylvania. She loves to learn about other cultures and go on adventures around the globe.

32